TURRIFF

A pictorial record of the town of Turriff

through the twentieth century including

local poetry and historical items

Published by
Turriff and District Heritage Society
2000

Published by

Turriff and District Heritage Society

The Auld Post Office Museum

24 High Street

Turriff, Aberdeenshire

AB53 4DS

Printed by:

W. Peters and Son Ltd.

16 High Street

Turriff, Aberdeenshire

AB53 4DT

ISBN 0-9539631-0-1

Copyright - 2000

Foreword

This book is a pictorial history of Turriff starting from the Auld Kirk, reputedly built in the eleventh century, through to the 1865 Cross of Turriff which rose from the ruins of the previous monument with its famous saying

"Choose ye, choose ye, at the Cross o' Turra, either gang to Aiberdeen or Elgin o' Moray."

Moving into the twentieth century we remember the Duncans of Hallhill, both father and son, who between them were the architects of many of our fine buildings including the Clydesdale Bank, Municipal Buildings, The Post Office, Turriff Hospital and many more.

Turriff has been very lucky in having had James Milne and William Gammie, two excellent local photographers. They have left a legacy of superb photographs of the parish taken from the early years of the century up to the fifties.

When Turriff Town Council stood down in 1975 to be replaced by the new Banff and Buchan District Council, many of the residents wanted to know what had become of the civic robes and regalia of their Town Council. After prolonged negotiations with Aberdeenshire Council, Turriff and District Heritage Society hope to have the robes and regalia back on display in the Auld Post Office Museum. Funds are currently being raised to purchase a special sealed glass case for the display of these items and it should be in place in time for the Spring opening of the museum in 2001.

The turn of the century has been highlighted with the Mart Arch in its new home and the Millennium Plaque completed beside the town centre garden.

A selection of the many poems about Turriff and its people has been included and at a later date the Society will publish a book of Turriff poems. I hope that this book will be of interest to all who either live in the area or have connections with it, not forgetting the Turriff expatriates around the world.

Bill Simpson

November 2000

'Turra'

A wee bit placie nestlin' doon
Wi burns and wids and hills a' roon,
It's hardly what ye'd ca' a toon,
    Oor native "Turra".
But little placie tho' it be,
It's dear tae you and dear tae me,
And prood we are tae say that we
    Were born and bred in "Turra".

The Auld Mill Chute, the Target Widdie,
The Deveron Brig whar we'd grow giddy.
The Green Gate and the Auld Brunt Smiddy
    Are dear tae a' frae "Turra".
The bonniest o' bonny spots
Frae far Land's End to "John o' Groats".
It's said that Mary Queen o' Scots
    Aince bade the nicht in "Turra".

We like tae think on the auld days
We ran aboot the Bracken Braes,
And climbed up trees and tore oor claes
    When we were loons in "Turra".
In summer time when days were hot,
A happy harum-scarum lot,
We dookit in the Rocky Pot,
    The public baths o' "Turra".

Then dressed in nature's first array,
We raced ower tae Kinnermit's Brae,
Or dried oorsels wi' wisps o' strae,
Upon the Haughs o' "Turra".
When Souter Hendry wi' his stick
Cam' on the scene, in half a tick
We'd disappeared sae michty quick,
    He flayed us loons in "Turra".

But "Turra" couldna' haud us aye,
And so at last there cam' a day
We had tae pairt, and we were wae
    Tae tak' the train frae "Turra".
Although it's got its Howe o' Hell,
And killin' hooses - sic a smell –
It's hame tae us, and heaven as well,
    Oor gweed auld-fashioned "Turra".

We like tae get the news frae hame,
And when we meet - whate'er his name –
The first thing spiered is aye the same,
    "When did ye hear frae "Turra?"
The weekly paper each discerns,
And in the local news soon learns
Fa's deid, fa's mairrit, and fa's got bairns,
    A thrivin' placie "Turra".

Some fairm's steadin's tae be "riggit",
Some braw new hooses tae be "biggit",
Some drain aboot the back roads "diggit",
    A clean-like placie "Turra".
The taxes aye on the increase,
Some fairmer has renewed his lease,
Some hawker fined for breach o' peace,
    That's a' the news in "Turra".

Historians say when at the "Trott",
The natives then a thrashin' got,
They threw their weapons on the spot,
    And ran awa' frae "Turra".
But Findlater, a native loon,
When shot in battle jist sat doon,
And blew his pipes and played a tune
    As if he'd been in "Turra".

And when the Queen, as jist she can,
Gied him the "Cross" wi' gracious han'
And said, "Far come ye frae, my man?"
    He proudly answered "Turra".
May Heaven frae a' bad things defend it,
And wi' a watchfu' e'e attend it,
Prosperity may He aye send it –
    Oor birthplace, "Turra".

Jamie Reid

The Cross of Turriff can be traced back to the mid-16th Century, but the foundation stone of the present cross was laid in December 1865.

It was designed and built by Turriff architect James Duncan, of Hallhill and some of the stones used in the previous cross are inside the one we see today. It also contained a bottle with the names of the local dignitaries of the day.

There is a rhyme associated with the cross which goes as follows "Choose ye, choose ye, at the Cross o' Turra, either gang to Aiberdeen or Elgin o' Moray".

On the far left of the photograph there once stood a building called Castle Rainy which was inhabited by a worthy called Lucky Rainy. Her claim to fame was the instructions she gave to her sons as they left home to make their way in the world. "Noo laddies tak tent, look after yersel, be sure that ye mak sillar – honestly if ye can, but mak it".

Castle Rainy was demolished in 1845 and eventually replaced by the Town Hall, built around the turn of the century which is the building shown on the left in the photograph.

OLD CHURCH GATE, TURRIFF

RUINS OF OLD CHURCH, TURRIFF

The Old Church, one of the sights of the town and now a picturesque ruin, was reputedly built by Malcolm Canmore during the eleventh century.

It is a long narrow building, 120 feet by 18 feet, with a handsome belfry tower containing a bell dated 1557.

Today only part of the building is roofed, but the tower clock is still operational.

The old churchyard contains many very old graves and reading the inscriptions can still give one an interesting insight into the people of Turriff two hundred years ago.

Turriff celebrating the Coronation of King George V and Queen Mary in 1911.

The Silver Band can be seen playing in the background.

The parade which started at the old Town Hall wound its way up High Street and through the town. The building on the left is the former Turriff Post Office designed by local architect James Duncan of Hallhill around the turn of the century and now the home of the Auld Post Office Museum.

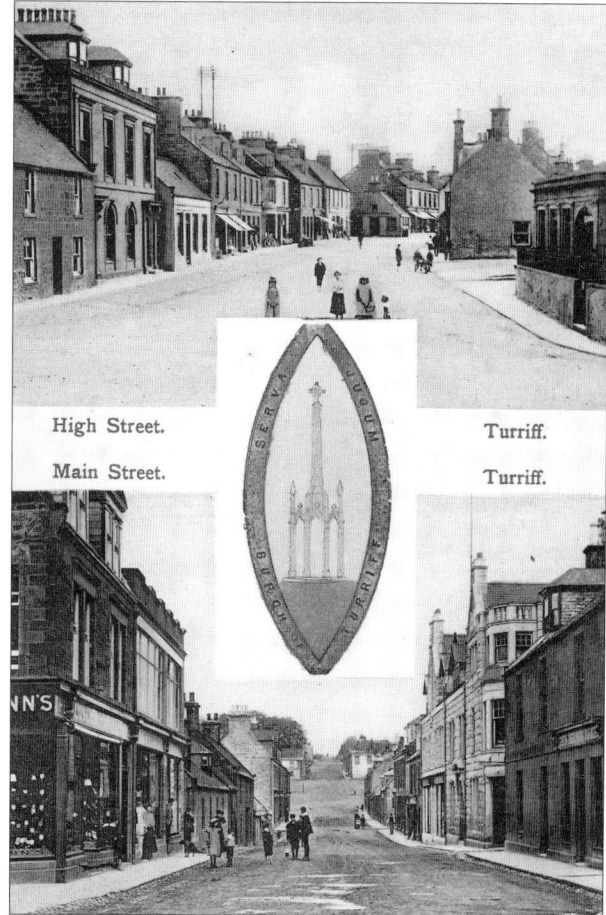

High Street.

Main Street.

Turriff.

Turriff.

Panoramic view of High Street and Main Street, Turriff in 1908 with the Town Logo and Motto superimposed in the middle of the postcard. Errol Lodging can be seen on the front right of the upper photograph. Double telephone poles on the left would indicate that the telephone system was already fairly advanced in Turriff. The lower view shows the Fife Arms Hotel on the right of the Square, looking remarkably similar to how it looks today. These two photograph postcards were very popular during the period prior to the First World War as you got two views for the price of one!

HIGH STREET, TURRIFF.

Another view of High Street, Turriff looking east, photographed in the late twenties. Turriff is changing, gas street lamps are starting to appear, the horse and cart is still the main mode of transport for goods but motor cars can be seen parked at the side of the street. Two gentlemen in business dress are crossing the street, probably heading for Hutcheons, by then a thriving wholesale grocery and agricultural supplies business. The building on the right of this photograph with the railings in the front is Turriff Town Council offices, designed by local architect James Duncan and erected in 1908.

TURRIFF HIGH STREET

High Street, Turriff looking west towards Castle Street, probably photographed in the thirties. Children heading for school in the morning, bright eyed and bushy tailed, I wonder how they looked on the way home at night? Motor transport is now fairly common. Davidson the Cycle Agent has added car repairs to his business and installed a Shell petrol pump on the pavement outside his shop. A motor cycle combination is waiting to be refuelled and a motor car is proceeding up the street, no parking problems in Turriff in those days!

High Street, Turriff

Post war view of High Street from the west in the early fifties. This looks like a market day in Turriff by the volume of traffic and shoppers. Most of the cars are of pre-war vintage as new vehicles were still in short supply at the time. Wm. Gammie, Newsagent and Bookseller can be seen on the right. Over a period of approximately fifty years Mr Gammie produced many of the Turriff photographic postcards which today still give us an insight into the town as it looked in the early twentieth century.

Mine Host at the Commercial Hotel before the First World War was Wilson Henry who operated a coach with four horses to transport guests to and from Turriff Railway Station. The Commercial Hotel changed hands several times prior to becoming the clubrooms of the Turriff Branch of the British Legion Scotland in the seventies.

Errol Lodging, situated at the corner of High Street and Station Road, this very substantial old building was once the Town House of the Earls of Errol who resided at Delgatie Castle. It later became the Bank House and had various occupants up to the 1970s when sadly it was demolished to make way for the widening of the main Aberdeen road into Turriff. Legend has it that there was once a tunnel which ran from Errol Lodging to Delgatie Castle. We sent a reporter from the Turriff Advertiser to investigate, so far she hasn't resurfaced at the castle!

The corner of High Street and Main Street where the first Episcopalian Chapel was built in 1739. The site was later redeveloped as the shops of William George, the Saddler, with Bob Anderson the Tinsmith next door. The property survived until the fifties when it was demolished and the site laid out as flowerbeds, creating a very attractive feature in the main thoroughfare through the town.

Main Street, Turriff looking north toward Markethill. Photograph from a Gammie postcard franked 1914. Gentleman in pony and trap probably heading for the railway station with his passenger, a well dressed lady with a large hat. Dunn's Shoe Shop on the left with a well stocked window of boots and shoes. On the right is Melvin the baker followed by the Union Hotel which has not changed very much over the years.

MAIN STREET TURRIFF

TURRIFF HONOURED AN ESTEEMED CITIZEN

Photo by L. P. Stephen Turriff.

Left to right. Major W. K. Leggat, of Yonderton (making the presentation); Mr N M Paterson, Mr Charles A. Duthie and Mr A. A. Reid.

Main Street, Turriff looking south in the late 40s. A horse and cart delivering milk can be seen outside the Union Hotel, health regulations were not so stringent at that time and the milk was dispensed straight from the cans into the customers' jugs or milk flagons. Austin 16 car parked by the pavement is probably the local hirer. C. Duthie & Sons, Plumbers, whose shop stood at the corner of Main Street and Chapel Street was a long established business. On his retirement in June, 1948, Charles Duthie was given a presentation by the community to mark his many years of public service. This included 51 years as Turriff Firemaster and 25 years as Captain of Turriff Boys' Brigade. His military service started as a Bugle Boy with the Volunteers in 1887, followed by the 5th Gordon Highlanders in the First World War and the Home Guard in the Second World War.

Main Street, Turriff looking north in the early fifties. Lyon's milk lorry can be seen coming out of the lane between Dunn's Shoe Shop and High Street where the dairy was situated. High Street and Main Street was the main route for vehicles passing through the town and was becoming increasingly congested by traffic and vehicles unloading, etc. Visibility on to High Street was greatly improved when the gable end building on the extreme left was demolished in the late fifties.

Early 60s photograph by Leslie Stephen of Main Street looking south. Mr Stephen's chemist and photography shop is on the corner of Main Street and Chapel Street. Left front is the china and haberdashery shop of James Barrie with the family home next door. Mr Barrie had two sisters, one of whom ran the shop while the other gave private piano lessons.

Johnston's Mart traded from a site near Turriff railway station when it was bought from Reith and Anderson in 1901. The original company name was Johnston and Paterson and the partners were Alexander Johnston and Robert Paterson (of Turra Coo fame). They closed the station premises and moved to Balmellie Street; Robert Paterson left the partnership in 1912. The Johnston family continued to run the business as one of the few privately owned marts until it was sold to Aberdeen and Northern Marts in 1954 and amalgamated with the Central Mart further along Balmellie Street. The Turriff marts were closed down in 1989.

Definitely a mart day in this view of Balmellie Street looking west, taken around 1913. In those days, before motor cars were widely used, the various travellers representing agricultural merchants from Aberdeen or Inverurie, would arrive at Turriff railway station with their bicycles in the goods van of the train. At the close of business at the mart they would cycle round some of their customers in the vicinity of the town before catching the train back to Aberdeen at night. Most of the houses in the forefront of the photograph were demolished to build Central Engineers on the left side and the Territorial Army Drill Hall on the right side of Balmellie Street.

School Lane, Turriff in the twenties looking north across what is now the car park, towards High Street. The roof and gable end of the Post Office can be seen centre right in the photograph. The milk cart delivered milk from Dorlaithers to Turriff daily.

Stephen Photo

FIFE STREET, TURRIFF. (10)

Fifties photograph of Fife Street looking west. The Alexanders bus from Aberdeen can be seen leaving Turriff, following the coastal route to Inverness, via Banff, Buckie and Elgin. The scenic road was a popular day trip for Aberdeen people during the summer holidays. Taking an Alexanders bus they would follow the coastal route up to Inverness in the morning, returning at night, either by train or the direct Inverness to Aberdeen bus which went via Keith.

STATION ROAD, TURRIFF,

Station Road looking north depicted on a Gammie photograph from 1927. The railway was the main carrier of freight at that time. Coal arrived at the station in bulk wagons where it was bagged before being transported by horse and cart, one of which can be seen toiling up Station Road with its heavy load, for delivery to the various coal merchants in Turriff and district. The rear of Errol Lodging, now demolished, can be seen on the right of the photograph.

Early thirties postcard published by Cruickshank, Chemist, Turriff showing the bottom half of Station Road looking north. The first house on the right is the Toll Cottage, still occupied today although it has been extended. The monumental masons yard and Granite Cottage, again both still in use and the granite balls remain on the entrance gate. On the high ground behind the Toll Cottage you can see Westwood House which was formerly a young ladies school known as Miss Wilson's Establishment which opened in the mid-nineteenth century. It is now a private residence.

Turriff Higher Grade School shown in a Gammie photograph from 1923. In 1879 a new school to accommodate 365 pupils was built on the site of the present Turriff Academy, this was extended in 1898. Turriff School was recognised as a higher grade establishment in 1904 and a technical department added in 1907. The old Academy was demolished during the sixties and a new Academy built in four phases at a cost of £533,610. It was officially opened on 21st October, 1971 by the late George Riddoch Wood, Freeman and former Provost of Turriff.

Victoria Terrace, Turriff, in 1909 looking west. On the right is Skene House followed by Clifton House and Clifton Cottage, all of which are still well maintained properties today. In the background is the old Turriff Academy which was demolished in the sixties to make way for the new and extended academy. The south side of Victoria Terrace is still agricultural land, some cultivated, the rest being used for grazing.

Rabbitie Jamie (Alias James Duff Duncan)

"Rabbitie" was born at Crossbrae, Delgaty in 1832. After a sparse education he made a living by doing messages for anybody who would employ him and eventually he managed to buy a horse and cab. He had by nature an extraordinary love of money and every penny was a prisoner. Many stories were told of the cunning and crafty manner in which he earned a livelihood and at one time he owned three horses. On his recovery after an acute mental illness, he posed as a sand vendor, having obtained, he thought, the sole right to a white sandpit at Delgaty. Jamie did not care to spend any of his money on food and clothing. These he managed to acquire on his rounds and his small earnings were regularly deposited in the bank.

It was a common sight to see "Rabbitie" trudging along the road pushing his wheelbarrow loaded with white sand. He obtained the sand at Woodside of Delgaty and covered a large area selling it to housewives to scour their pots and milk churns with, and receiving lots of presents and pieces along the way. It is said that some of the housewives were "jist a wee bit feart" at Jamie and often gave him bits of presents to get rid of him. Jamie had a great aversion to being called "Map" and used to say "I dinna mind them ca'in me Rabbitie, but I canna stand Map".

The schoolchildren would torment him by running up behind and shouting, "Rabbitie, Rabbitie", which he ignored, but if they shouted "Map", he would drop the barrow and chase them, They usually scattered in all directions and he had little chance of catching them and would shake his fist and vow vengeance at a later date.

Jamie lived in a "wee hoosie" near the Market Hill in Turriff and the young men often gave him a call on their way into Turriff in the evening. On one occasion a few young fellows entered his house and found him in bed. "O Jamie" said one, "Ye're early beddit the nicht. Are ye weel eneuch?" "Oh, ay", said Jamie, "I'm rael weel, but I hardly got ony sleep yestreen. The left e'e did sleep a wee filie, bit the richt e'e niver shut ava."

"Rabbitie" was 64 when he died and he had been missing for eight weeks before his body was found. His gravestone in the Auld Kirkyard bears the following inscription:

In Memory of James Duff Duncan, "Rabbitie", an eccentric character, whose body was recovered from the Deveron near Muiresk House, on 3rd April, 1896. "Aye livin' ".

The latter quotation, his usual reply to "How are you?"

Francie Markis (Francis Jamieson)

Born in the parish of New Deer in the year 1823, Francis Jamieson was the son of William Jamieson, who moved from the district of Deer to the hills of Fisherie in 1834. In 1837 the family were in such reduced circumstances that on 23rd March, William Jamieson appealed for help, whereupon the Rev. Mr Findlay, King Edward, "gave him a shilling". Possessed of a native wit bordering on genius, the family clowned their way through Buchan for half a century. At fairs and markets, barn dances and social functions, Francis Jamieson, "Francie Markis", his nephew Joe Sim, the "Wonderful Boy", and Jean Jamieson, who bore the picturesque title of the "heel wadge", dominated the rural scene. The old clay biggin' No. 45 Hill o' Cook, where Francie held court to all from far and near, no longer exists, but its site and the garden remains. It is said that when his father built the house at Hill of Cook, he first cut the trees on the site, then built their home around the tree stumps in order to use them as chairs!

A worthy of the highest order, Francie is said to have acquired the name of "Markis" when a visitor to the family croft at Hill of Cook asked to see him. Francis was away at Macduff that day with a load of peats pulled by his oxen and Mrs Jamieson is quoted as saying "If you meet him on the road ye canna miss him, he's a great big chiel, just like a marquis".

He excelled at running, jumping, throwing the hammer, putting the stone, slinging the weight, pulling the sweirtree and wrestling. With ridiculous effrontery, he raced the train between Turriff and Macduff at the opening of the new line, he challenged all comers and was seldom beaten. A natural musician, he excelled at the bagpipes and the bass fiddle. He played and sang, displaying amazing ability. He ate prodigiously. Dozens of eggs, raw and boiled, "to give some variety to the feast", scones, biscuits, gingerbread, treacle, and a pound of butter, was the preliminary to devouring a turkey, and great draughts of raspberry ale. Sparrows baked in clay were a special delicacy, he ate them feathers and all! For a bet he would pluck a hen and eat it raw, "guts as weel". In his primitive dwelling, fowls roosting on the rafters could direct a well placed shot of excreta into the wooden bowl, as Francie stood stirring his brose. With characteristic humour, he declared that this gave his brose a special flavour.

To facilitate his progress, he took to careering through the countryside on stilts. Timid in the dark and superstitious to a degree, he nevertheless inspired awe in the very young. The vision of Francie tearing along like some gigantic wraith, was enough to make the most precocious child seek the shelter of its cot.

As the years progressed, he became a byeword and a legend. His ready wit, pawky sayings and manner of dress, made him the supreme oddity. He resented the encroachment of age that cramped his style, but his interest in athletics and music remained unabated. During his last years he knew again the pinch of poverty. When he died on the 19th of September 1903, the bass fiddle that was part of him, his tramp pick, double lever watch, and treasured telescope were no longer in his possession. He is buried in the new cemetery at Byth.

Francie (Marquis) House, Cruden, Turriff.

Cockie O' Turra
(Alias John Williamson)

Cockie was born in a croft at Delgaty in 1841 but moved to Turriff as a child to stay with his mother and grandmother. He attended school but did not learn a great deal, some said he "wanted tuppence in the dozen", but what he lacked in learning he made up for in native wit.

He became the town crier and bill poster and was a familiar sight in the streets of Turriff for many years, dressed in his old volunteers uniform with the bell in one hand and his bucket of batter and brush in the other.

When he died he was buried in the Auld Kirkyard and his grave bears the following inscription:

"Erected by public subscription to the memory of John Williamson, "Cockie", for 30 years town crier in Turriff; died February 1892 aged fifty years, "Ye winna forget me fan I'm awa."

The poem "Cockie O' Turra" which was written by John S. Rae, really says it all and is essential reading for all Turriff expatriates and natives, young and old.

This poem was written several years before Cockie died and was widely circulated at the time, selling for one penny per copy. Cockie, under his real name of John Williamson, pushed the sale of them with great gusto as all the proceeds went to him.

Wha e'er has been to Turra toon
Has seen, nae doot that famous loon
Wha blaws the horn and beats the drum
An' intimates events to come.
Aye followed by a crew o' geets
This worthy trots along the streets
Intent on postin' bills wi' batter
Made by himsel wi' flour an' water.
When roused he turns upon the loons
An' soundly claws their wicked croons
Nae for the reason that they're yockie
But just because they ca' him Cockie.
When shows an' circuses come roon
He pilots them into the toon
An' shows the Black Bull as they pass
For weel he likes a reamin' glass.
He tells them o' the Howe o' Hell
And warns them to be aware o' Nell
Whose towsie heid an' fearsome face
Has scared the rottins from the place.
On market days upon the hill
He coups fu' mony a glass an' gill
Till he can neither stan' or stutter
But like a ba' rows i' the gutter.
An grunts an' groans wi' micht an' main
An' vainly tries tae rise again
While impish loons wi' faces jockey
Pelt him wi' dubs an' bawl oot "Cockie".
In Turra Toon for mony a year
Has lived this worthy, quaint an' queer
An' Turriffites where e're they've gone
Delight to hear the tricks o' John
Thus "Cockie" wi' his brush an' batter
Gangs on through life wi' rantin' clatter
An' though nae 'soun' he'll hae his day
Like ither men o' mortal clay.

After the death of Cockie a book was published called **Brief Reminiscences of John Williamson "Cockie".** It contained many anecdotes on his life and ended with the following poem also written by John S. Rae.

A LAMENT FOR "COCKIE"

Auld Turra weel may claw her heid,
An' greet her 'een a' bleert an' red;
Her greatest son, alas, is deid –
    Puir John's awa.
Nae mair we'll hear his Scryin Screed,
    Nor's horn blaw.
Frae Market hill to Gaswark's brae,
The loons are lookin' blate an' wae,
They feel a blank in life's by play,
    Since "Cockie's" deid;
For John's fierce charge could clear the way
    Wi' wondrous speed.
Nae mair they'll flee wi' dinsom clatter;
An' John ahin wi' brush an' batter;
Their grinin' ranks to charge an' scatter,
    O'er street or lea;
For John when roused could end the matter
    As brisk's a bee.
Nae mair the comin' wild beasts show
Will "Cockie" scry to high an' low,

Nor ride the elephants fu' slow,
    On circus days;
Nor offer monkeys snuff, he! ho!
    Nor nip their taes.
Nae mair the fatal "tippence" nip
Will lay John on his back or hip
Nor gar him i' the gutters dip
    His classic nose;
While swayin' like a storm tossed ship,
    When tempest blows.
Alas, we'll hear his voice nae mair
Resoundin' loud on Street or Square;
He's done wi' brush an' batter ware,
    An' urchin's jokey.
A better place an' better fare,
    This day has "Cockie."
Ye Turriff loons lang mind his face,
His brush an' pail, an' wondrous dress;
There's nae anither o' his race
    In a' your Burgh.
John's left mair than the maist o' us
– A blank in Turra.

This proud gentleman not only went along to Wm Gammie the photographer at 15 High Street, to have his picture taken, but brought along his new bicycle to be snapped at the same time.

To date the photograph, we consulted a vintage cycle expert who advised that the machine was probably an Ariel in fashion around 1900.

These early cycles were made to measure with a frame to suit the stature of the owner being fitted before it left the factory. Features included, double crossbar, toolbag attached to rear of seat, caliper brakes and carbide lamp.

The present St Congan's Church in Turriff was consecrated by Bishop Suther on 24th October, 1867. It was built using materials from the former Episcopal Church in Schoolhill.

The pulpit was placed in memory of John Duguid Milne of Melgum, and Barbara, his wife, by their children. The lectern was given in memory of Mary, widow of William Urquhart of Craigston by her grandchildren. A window in memory of Sir Robert Abercromby of Birkenbog was erected by his widow and children.

St Andrew's Church was previously known as Turriff Free Church, it opened for worship in June 1900 and was built on the site of a previous church dating back to 1844. Built with a rich coloured sandstone from the Hatton Quarries, the church cost £2500 and the congregation already had £2100 in hand before the work of building had commenced. At the time of building a memorial stone was incorporated containing a sealed box, the contents of which included old newspapers from the previous church memorial stone and a statement of the proceedings in connection with the building of the church. Photographs of Rev. Dr Sutherland, Rev. R. S. Simpson and Rev. William Logan were also enclosed.

The new Parish Church was built on the site of a previous church in 1794. In 1914 it re-opened after two years closure for major renovation both inside and out at a cost of £3250.00. The official re-opening ceremony was carried out by the Moderator of the General Assembly, the Right Reverend Professor Nicol, D.D., on 14th August 1914, the day that Britain declared war on Germany and the First World War started. The name of the church was changed to the "Parish Church of St Ninian's, Turriff", in 1937. With the union of St Ninian's and Forglen Parish Church in 1971 the name became "St Ninian's and Forglen Parish Church". To mark the 200th anniversary of the church in 1995 it was visited by the Moderator of the General Assembly of the Church of Scotland the Right Reverend James Harkness.

"Porter Fair"
(Turriff Feeing Market, 1884)

Porter Fair in 1871 from a photograph by Milne. High Street is thronging with farm workers eager to get a "fee" for six months, or if they were lucky, perhaps twelve months work. The Fair was held twice a year, at the May and November terms. Farm servants came from far and near to meet up with the farmers who were looking for horsemen, cattlemen, halflins or kitchen maids. Porter Fair was still in existence in the mid-thirties but died out before the start of the Second World War.

The term time wi' merry May
Has come again ance mair
An' a' the lads an' lasses gay
Are gaun to Porter Fair.

Frae a' the roads they're troopin' in,
In jovial crowds sae rare;
The country lad is far ahin'
That's nae at Porter Fair.

The ploughman loon, sae brisk an' braw
This day is free o' care;
He'll see his merry cronies a'
Again at Porter Fair.

It's nae sae aft he has a day,
An' ready cash to spare;
Nae wonder that his spirit's gay
Wi thochts o' Porter Fair.

The sweetie stan's alang the streets
Display their temptin' ware;
An' mony ither grander treats
Are seen at Porter Fair.

The country laddies hug an' kiss
Their sonzie lasses there,
An' ither things that are amiss
They dae at Porter Fair.

In crowded inns, the "barley bree"
Gi'es wings to a' his care–
The ploughman's fairly on the spree
This day at Porter Fair.

Blin' fiddlers scrape wi' a' their micht
The cat-gut an' the hair,
To dancers reelin' wrang an' richt
In crowds at Porter Fair.

An' warblers o' the Tinker train,
Wi lungs o' vigour rare,
Sing deeds of old in warlike strain
To stir up Porter Fair.

They hoarsely shout o' mony a field
O' battle teuch an' sair,
Where Scotland's foes aye backward reel'd,
Though thick as Porter Fair.

The feein' too gaes briskly on
Wi burly famers there;
They ken he's aye a decent loon
They fee at Porter Fair.

They ken he'll ploo' a bonnie rig,
An' o' their horse tak' care;
An' sae they fee him, clean an' trig,
That day at Porter Fair

The day noo ower, they hameward plod–
The lads an' lasses fair,
An' troth it is a merry road
That leads frae Porter Fair.

The lads half-fou the lasses lo'e,
An' for them ocht wad dare,
Aye vowin true, wi' mou' to mou',
The nicht o' Porter Fair.

Nor will they part, they are sae fain,
Ilk ardent loving pair,
Till dawn proclaims the day again
That follows Porter Fair.

John S. Rae
Burngrains, Alvah.

THEN AND NOW
THE CHANGING FACE OF TURRIFF

An update of business premises and occupiers in Main Street and High Street, as they were seventy-five years ago and as they are today

Main Street from the Square

East Side		West Side	
1925	**2000**	**1925**	**2000**
Mitchell's Baker & Grocer	McKenzie, Baker	Annie Smart's Sweet Shop	Alldays Grocery Store
A. Arioni Ice Cream Shop	H. Orlandi, Ice Cream Shop	Simon Shoemaker	Bain Henry Reid, Accountants
Stuart Tailor Shop	Brian's of Turriff, Gent's Outfitters	Brown Cabinetmaker	Junior Celebrations
Stuart Tailor Workshop	Dolphin Fish & Chip Bar	To Pearson's Nurseries	To Sim Gardens
Barrie China Shop	Magpies, Furniture Store	Cranna Shoemaker	Cranna Shoemaker
Barrie's House	Jungle Mania, Pet Shop	Rankin Draper	Scotch Corner Kilt Shop
Rankin's Mens Shop	Gibson Ross, Chemist	" "	Nickel & Dime Store
C. Duthie Plumber	KJs Haberdashery	Joe Rae Joiner	Petit Deli Sandwich Shop
Fewtrell Chemist	"The flower Shop", Helen Taylor	Booth's Dairy	A. E. Brown & Son, Butchers
Ledingham Painter	Celebrations Department Store	Simpson Miller & Grocer	Victoria Wine Lodge
Hutcheon Saddler	" " " "	Barron Hirer	Demolished
R. Hay Grocer	" " " "	Fraser Barber	Lloyds TSB (Scotland) Bank
W. Reid Draper	" " " "	Craik Butcher	Porters Bakery Shop
Union Hotel	Union Hotel	" "	Deveron Sports
Melvin Baker	A. Youngson (Turriff) Ltd.	" "	Sue Ryder Shop
North of Scotland Bank	Clydesdale Bank	Chalmers Ironmonger	Wheels, Cycle Shop
		Wiseman Tailor	Piazola's Italia Restaurant
		Dunn's Shoe Shop	Stewart & Watson Property Shop

High Street from the Cross

South Side		North Side	
1925	**2000**	**1925**	**2000**
Errol Lodging	Safeway Supermarket	Miss Terrace Fancy Shop	Demolished for road widening
Hutcheons Agricultural Merchants	" " "	Town and County Bank	Stewart & Watson, Solicitors
Anderson's Black Bull Inn	" " "	Taylor Equitable	Atholl Scott, Accountants
Annie Hay's Toy & Sweet Shop	" " "	" "	Lifestyle, Ladies' Fashions
Watson Painter	Entrance to new car park	Greenlees Shoe Shop	Johnston & Carmichael, Accountants
Stephen Tailor	" " "	Davidson Cycle Agent	" " " " "
Municipal Offices	Municipal Offices	Milne Chemist & Photographer	R. S. McColl, Newsagents
Post Office	The Auld Post Office Museum	Pratt, Saddler	Fiona's Pantry, Coffee Shop
Simpson's Tea Rooms	Wong's Kitchen, Chinese Take-Away	Telephone Exchange	House
Cassie Butcher	Cassie Butcher	J. Gordon Shoemaker	Nan Anderson, Ladies' Fashions
McKenzie Jeweller	Geddes (Turriff Jewellers)	Davidson Watchmaker & Jeweller	" " " "
McDonald's Workshop	Turf Accountants	Stewart Baker & Grocer	J. Stewart (Turriff) Ltd. (Costcutter)
McDonald's Tailor	W. Peters & Son Ltd., Printers & Stationers	Smith Shoemaker	Demolished
Morrison's (Law's) Grocer	White Heather Hotel	Davidson Hairdresser	" "
Shand Draper	Brown & McRae, Solicitors	Scroggie Shoemaker	Hislop, Shoe Shop
Alfie Davidson Butcher	A. J. Stewart, Dentist	Porter Grocer	D. & L. Beedie, Newsagents
Chalmers Grocer (later Co-op)	" "	Miss Knox Laundry	D. Cruickshank, Photographer
Cruickshank Chemist	A. S. Cruickshank, Chemist	Tommy Kemp Cycle Agent	" "
Commercial Hotel (Wilson Henry)	Royal British Legion Social Club	Milne Shoemaker	Lucas Service UK Ltd.
		" "	" "
		" "	Flowers 'n' Things, Flower Shop
		Christie Draper	Alliance & Leicester Building Society
		" "	Tangles Hair Salon
		Gammie Newsagent & Photographer	Bank of Scotland
		Union Bank	" "
		Commercial Bank	Royal Bank of Scotland
		Bob Anderson Tinsmith	Municipal flower beds
		George The Saddler	" " "

Golf Pavilion, Turriff.

Turriff Golf Club was formed in 1896 and played on a site at Markethill until 1925 when they moved to Rosehall. A nine hole course was laid out which was extended to eighteen holes in 1976. The present clubhouse shown in the photograph was built in 1938, extended in 1973 and again in 1992. Popular professional of the Turriff Golf Club from 1934 to 1977 was Davie Shepherd. His daughter, Pat, carried on the family tradition, winning the Turriff Ladies' Golf Championship for the first time in 1958, continuing the winning sequence unbroken for thirty years to 1988, a feat which led to her being recognised in the Guinness Book of Records, one of the few records by a Scot that the book contains.

The Bridge of Deveron at Turriff from a Milne photograph of 1905. The trees are quite sparse compared with today and the Toll Cottage stands in its original position, nearer the bridge. The bridge was built in 1826 to replace a ferry. It was also known as the Eastside Bridge because the toll for crossing was paid at the Toll Cottage on the east bank of the Deveron (the Turriff side of the river).

Turriff Station in 1913. The railway line from Inveramsay to Turriff opened in 1857 and was extended to Macduff in 1860. The line was closed to passenger traffic in 1951 and ceased goods carriage at Turriff on 3rd January, 1966. The Station Yard has been converted into a busy caravan site but part of the platform can still be seen and the station sign is in the Auld Post Office Museum in Turriff. The last stationmaster was Charles Simpson who also looked after Fyvie Station. The tall chimney in the background is the Old Meal Mill now converted into modern flats.

DELGATY CASTLE, TURRIFF.

Gammie, Photo.

Delgatie Castle, situated two miles east of Turriff, is a massive L planned tower with battlements and turrets. It consists of five storeys and is over sixty feet high. The original building dates back to 1579, with extensions in the 17th century and wings added in the 18th and 19th century. Much of the modern renovation was done by the late Captain John Hay of Delgaty who died in September 1997. The castle is now run by a trust and is open to the public.

Hatton Castle lies two and a half miles south-east of Turriff. This castellated mansion was largely rebuilt and modernised by Mr Garden Duff in 1814. It became the family residence of the Garden Duffs, replacing Balquholly House. Hatton Castle is largely surrounded by mature trees, making it a very sheltered and desirable site for a home. Present Laird of Hatton is David James Duff.

The present Craigston Castle was built by John Urquhart the "Tutor of Cromarty" who died at Craigston in 1631 and is buried at King Edward Church. The castle completed in 1607, stands over sixty feet high with very thick walls and turrets and remains in good condition today. Craigston Castle is still in the possession of the Urquharts who are descendants of the "Tutor of Cromarty".

Craigston Castle, Turriff.   Gammie, Photo.

GAMMIE PHOTO   NEW HOUSE CARNOUSIE, TURRIFF

The New House of Carnousie. This fine mansion designed by Archibald Simpson in the Palladian style was built on a terrace above the existing Carnousie House by Captain Grant. When he died in 1842 the house although outwardly complete, had not been internally fitted out and the windows were boarded up. His successor Mr W J Harvey decided against occupying it and instead extended the existing Carnousie House. The New House remained empty and neglected for many years. It was eventually sold to Aberdeen University, who demolished it and used the granite in the building of Elphinstone Hall at Kings College.

FORGLEN HOUSE, TURRIFF.
Photo by MILNE, TURRIFF.

A 1907 photograph of Forglen House Turriff. It was designed by John Smith and built in 1845 to replace an earlier house on the same site. Forglen House is the former home of the Abercrombys, whose family mausoleum built in 1852, still stands in the policies of the estate. There is also a monument built in 1853 in memory of the members of the Abercromby family who died in the Crimean War.

A 1906 view of Muiresk House, Turriff on a postcard by Milne of Turriff. Parts of the house are pre-1604, the west wing was built in 1700 and a further wing added during the eighteenth century. Muiresk is still a private residence and the policies include fishing on the River Deveron.

Balquholly House was built by the Duffs of Hatton. Work commenced in 1891 but the house was not completed until 1898, the name Balquholly comes from a burn which flows near Hatton. The Duffs gifted the house to their daughter on the occasion of her marriage but it was later sold to the Tweedales. In 1924 Robert Paterson of Lendrum bought the Estate, which was later inherited by his son George who resided at Balquholly until the fifties.

DUNLUGAS HOUSE, TURRIFF.

Dunlugas House, Turriff pictured in a Gammie photograph of 1906. The house was built in 1793 and the pedimented central bay, framed by quoins, contains a double pilastered entrance at the head of a flight of stairs with a bullseye window at the top. Formerly the home of the Ogilvies and the Abercrombys, it is now a private residence.

Photograph taken at C.R. McLeod's engineering workshop at Clifton Lane, Turriff in the late twenties. It shows Turriff District Committee's first combined tar sprayer mounted on a steam road roller. L-R back row – Dod Rattray, Alex Wilson (Findon), Alex Kelman, George Fordyce. L-R front row – Jamie Taylor, Willie Alexander, Jack Rae, Sidney Smith, Frank Geddes.

Steam traction engine driving a stone crusher for road metal at Aberdeenshire County Council quarry at St John's Wells, Fyvie in 1938. Engine driver is Jack Wilson (Forglen).

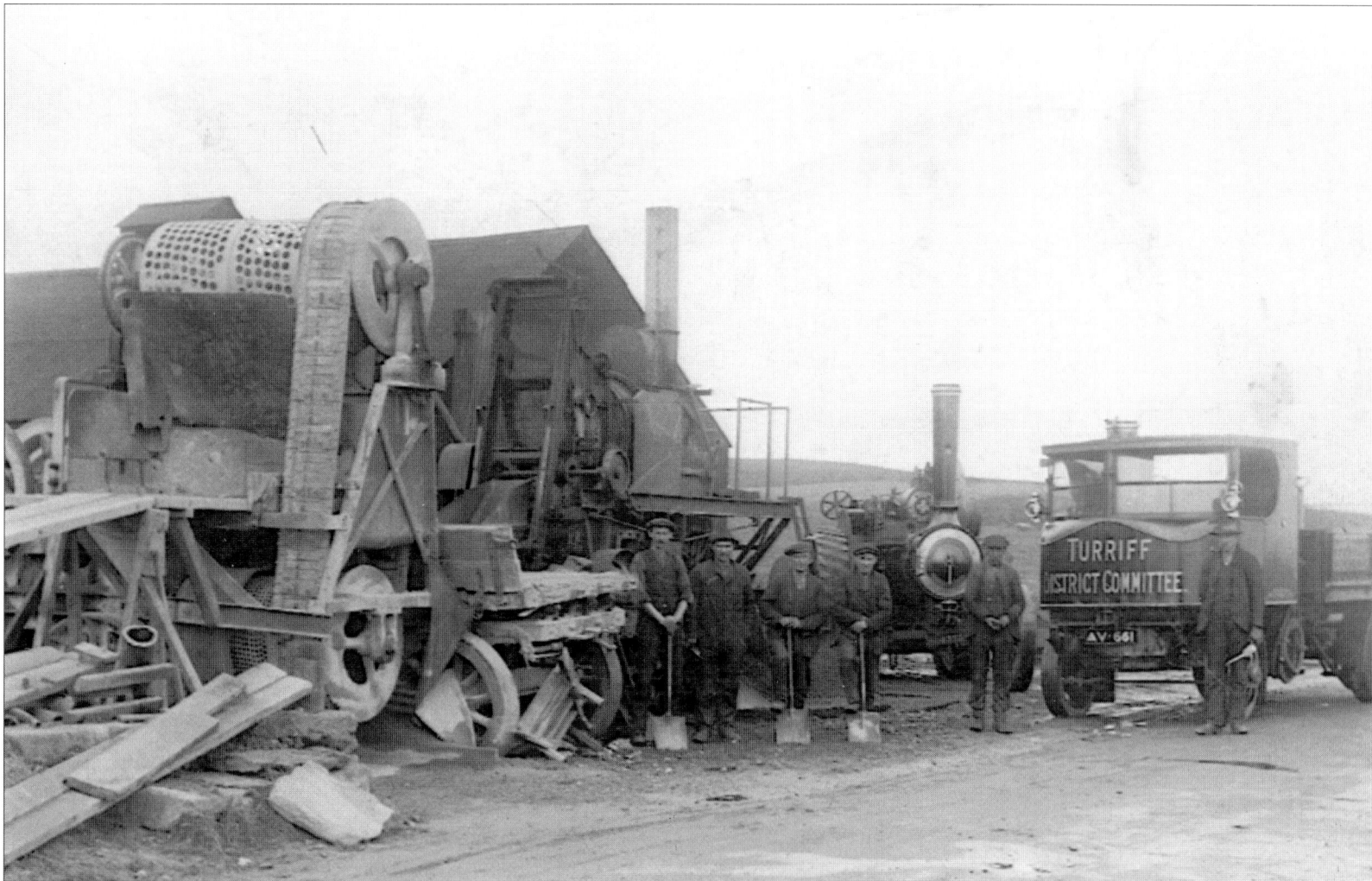

Turriff District Committee's depot at Millmoss Turriff, in the late twenties . Stone was brought to the yard for breaking down to road metal by the crusher which was driven by a steam traction engine. As there were not many quarries in the Turriff area suitable for road metal, some of the stones cleared from fields by farmers were collected and used at Millmoss for crushing. The depot was also used for storage of equipment and road rollers etc. In later years Turriff District Committee became part of Aberdeenshire County Council Roads Department.

The last goods train from Macduff to Aberdeen pictured at Turriff Station on 1st August 1961. The porter on the left is Sandy Hepburn. The photograph was taken by 13-year-old Robert Milne who was the only person at the station to meet the train. Robert is better known today as the local Admin. Director of the charity organisation No Frontiers who regularly transport relief supplies of food and clothing from Aberdeen to Yugoslavia for the people of Kosovo.

The Central Mart opened on its present site in 1887, the arched doorway was added in 1899. Along with Johnston's Mart it gave Turriff livestock sales three days each week. This helped the town to become one of the main livestock auction sales centres outside Aberdeen. In 1954 it was amalgamated with Johnston's Mart and continued until 1989 when both marts were closed. After demolition of the Central Mart site in the 90s, the arch was preserved and is now the gateway to the east entrance to the Den.

The picture shows the local cinema which was opened in 1937 and was extremely popular, open on Mondays, Wednesdays and Saturdays, and was open nightly during World War II. The building was originally the Town Hall and was used then for dances, concerts and public functions, but low usage closed it and it became a cinema. When television arrived cinemas started to close and it became a furniture showroom , then a fancy goods showroom and cafe and is now a nightclub.

'D' Company 5th Gordon Highlanders leaving Turriff Station en route for France on Thursday, 6th August, 1914, at the start of the First World War. Many of the soldiers came from Turriff district which was a strong recruiting area for the Territorial Battalions of the Gordon Highlanders.

Photograph of staff and patients at Turriff VAD Hospital for servicemen which was in St Andrew's Church Hall during the First World War. Front row, third from right is Dr Niven and on his right are Rachael Ainslie Grant Duff of Delgatie Castle and on her right is the matron of the hospital.

Erroll Road, Turriff in the sixties. The gentleman with the bicycle is Robert Barron who ran the Post Office and tailors shop at Kirktown of Auchterless. He is seen leaving the home of his son Bill Barron, who for many years was the burgh gardener, responsible for maintaining the local recreation grounds.

Members and officials of Turriff Town Council in the early 1960s. L-R – Douglas Turnbull (Burgh Surveyor) A M Fordyce, Adam Simpson (Town Clerk), Dr David Hogg, James Dawson (Senior Bailie), Ben Thomson, George Riddoch Wood (Provost), Andrew Finlayson, George Fowlie (Treasurer), William Robertson.

1954 photograph of Turriff Silver Band. Back row – L-R G Fordyce, A Leith, J Russell, A Fowlie, F Taylor, J Kerr, G Innes, F Cranna. Middle row – L-R A Leith, G Innes, A Mackie, A Paterson, J Cranna, A Sim, G Wilson, A McDonald. Front row – L-R L McIntosh, A Mutch, W Mollison, G Fordyce, I Smith, W Mollison, J Chalmers. Earliest record of Turriff Silver Band is 1914 but little information is available from then up to the 1950s. During this period Mr G C Fordyce was the band's long serving conductor. In 1954 the band played in the Scottish Championships in Edinburgh and gained first place in the fourth section. The band was invited to play at Macduff Harbour in 1961 for the arrival of the Queen and the Duke of Edinburgh in the Royal Yacht Britannia. With Bill Barron as conductor, the band was again successful at the Scottish Championships in 1986, gaining third place in the fourth section and at the national finals in 1996 the band gained second place in the fourth section of the Scottish Championships with Moira Ross as conductor. This gained them promotion to the third section and the opportunity to play in the National Finals in Cardiff. The Turriff musicians won the third section of the Scottish Championships in 1999 and competed in the National Finals in Nottingham gaining promotion to the second section, an achievement that has given the band the most successful period of its history.

Turriff and District Pipe Band proceeding along Main Street in the early 1950s. The nucleus of the original band was formed by ex-servicemen on their return from the trenches of the First World War, the inaugural meeting being held in 1923. In 1998 the band celebrated 75 years of distinction, both as a body and individually, in fields of regional and national competition. On the extreme left of the front rank in the picture is Pipe Major George Hepburn representing a family name synonymous with the Turriff and District Pipe Band. On the extreme right is his son, Pipe Sergeant Bill Hepburn. It is quite remarkable that in over 75 years since the formation of the band they have had only five Pipe Majors in that time, a quite unique record: William Scott 1923, Eric Findlater 1923-27, George Findlater V.C. 1927-40, George Hepburn 1940-70, William Hepburn 1970 ongoing. Pipers (L-R) Pipe Major George Hepburn, Kenny Steel, Harry Fraser, Pipe Sgt., Bill Hepburn, John Robertson, Angus McAllister, Bill Maitland. Bass section – George Murray, Sandy Bowie, Eddie Smith, Andy Fraser. Drummers (back row) Robert Wilson, ? Bowie, Dougie Ogston.

Thirteen past presidents of Turriff Bowling Club pictured in 1978. L-R – George Strachan, Jack Davidson, Alex Brown, Sandy Benzie, Pat Gaul, Charles Taylor, John Ledingham, Sandy Forbes, Willie Finnie, Robert Fraser, Sandy Florence, Charles Angus, William Murray. Turriff Bowling Club was established in 1878 and in 1887 a disused sand quarry was purchased and the present green laid out at a cost of £33.13.6. Current membership of the club is approximately 500 and the president for 2000-2001 is Norman Donaldson. In 1952 members decided they needed a building where they could play indoor bowls and at an extraordinary general meeting of the club it was agreed to purchase a used wooden tearoom for £450.00. This was transported to the site, rebuilt and the conversion completed in 1953, giving the club three carpets for indoor play at a cost of £2,000.00. By 1977 the clubhouse was in need of massive repairs and members voted to build a full rink stadium which was completed in 1978 at a cost of £90,000.00.

Municipal Recreation Grounds in Balmellie Road around the late 40s. Residents and visitors alike could enjoy putting, tennis and bowling. Turriff Tennis Club also had their private tennis courts nearby.

QUEEN'S ROAD, TURRIFF

Queen's Road in the late 60s prior to the Gateway Community Centre and Turriff Swimming Pool being opened in 1973. The gasometer of the old gasworks can be seen on the left of the photograph. The manufacture of coal gas started in Turriff around 1839 with the formation of a joint stock company with shore capital of £750.00. Supplies of coal for the manufacturing process was transported from the nearby railway station by horse and cart. In 1842 gas consumption in the town was 188,000 cubic feet for the year.

HOWE OF MILLMOSS, TURRIFF.

Gammie, Photo.

An unusual view looking east from Turriff, across the Water of Idoch towards Millmoss Farm in the centre of the picture. On the right is the Old Meal Mill with its distinctive chimney. A line of railway cattle wagons can be seen parked on the railway siding behind the building. These were used to accommodate cattle from the annual sales being sent south. The photograph probably dates from the fifties when the Mill was owned by the North of Scotland Milling Company.

The Turra Show

They come, they come, frae ilka side
Frae a the country roon.
They're streamin in a human tide
Tae far famed Turra toon.
Aboon the cloods an August sun
Teets oot an says "Hullo"
I think I'll tak a holiday
An bide at Turra Show.

There's fairmers frae the Banks o Don
There's ploomen frae the Dee.
An shepherds frae the Tap o Noth
An the Spittal o Glenshee.
There's folk frae aff the Cabrach hills
Wha dwell amang the snow.
For folk frae a the warld o'er
Ye'll see at Turra Show.

The settin noo - the Turra Haughs –
Twas made by nature's hand.
It's dottit ower wi motor cars
An charabangs and prams.
Ploos and kye,
Machines that reap and sow.
For onything worth lookin at
It's there at Turra Show.

There's tents crammed foo wi eggs and cheese,
An flooers that are sublime.
Ye'd think ye were enterin Paradise
But it's Turra a the time.
The kale, the neeps, the record beets,
An scones tae mak ye grow,
An rhubarb stalks like mountain pines,
They're a at Turra Show.

Then fin the sun gangs ower the hill
Saft blaws the evenin breeze –
There's music a roon Turra toon
An love amang the trees!
An as ye turn yer heid for hame
Ye murmer as ye go –
The greatest scene in a the land's
The Turra Summer Show.

Ben Thomson Senior **c 1950**

Turriff Show in the 90s. A sunny day for Turriff Show with the crowds flocking to the Haughs to view the wide variety of exhibits and watch the ring programme. The first Turriff Show was held in 1864 on the Market Hill where it continued until 1924 before moving to the Haughs. The year 2000 saw the 136th Show of the Turriff Agricultural Association.

PLEASURE WALK, TURRIFF,

Gammie, Phot

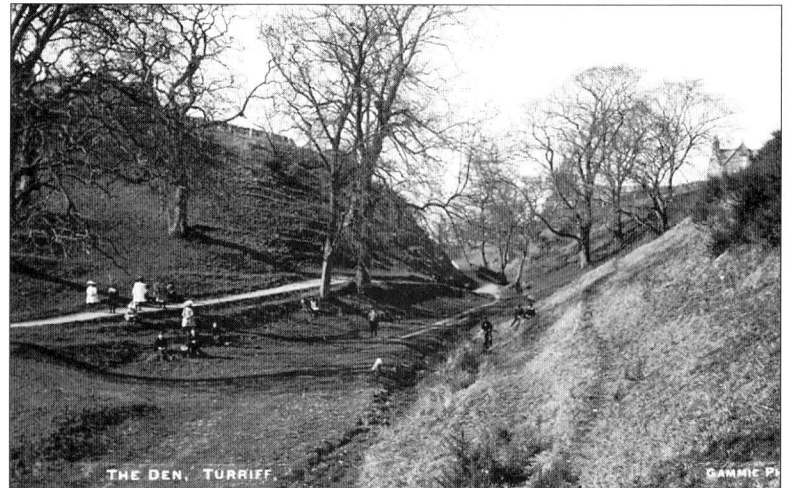

THE DEN, TURRIFF.

GAMMIE P

The Den Turriff on Gammie photographs from the early twenties. Today this municipal park is a popular venue for picnics and outings with its boating pond and children's playground. The trees have now matured and there are lovely walks along the braes. It has also been the home of the famous Turriff Show since 1924.

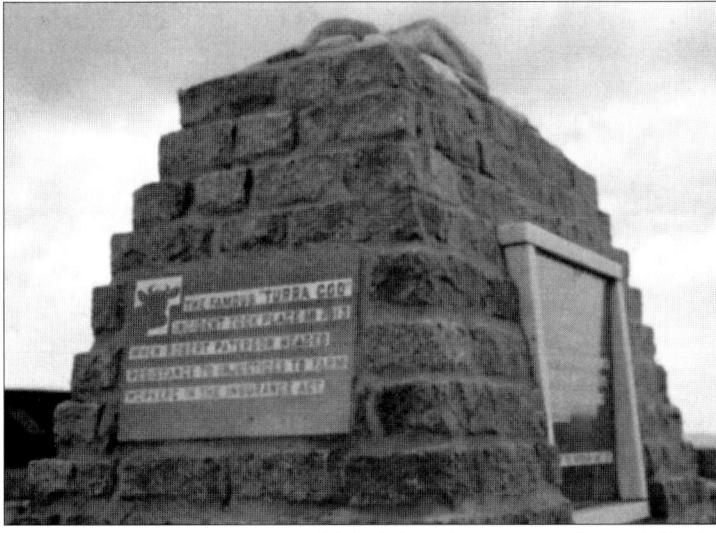

The Square Turriff in the late 40s. In 1913 it was at the centre of the 'Turra Coo' incident when a riot ensued at the attempted sale of Robert Paterson's cow which had been poinded when the owner protested against the National Health Act by withholding payment of National Insurance contributions for his employees. It was later auctioned in Aberdeen and bought by local farmers who presented it back to Mr Paterson. A memorial to the 'Turra Coo' can be seen at Lendrum Farm, Auchterless, the original home of the famous 'coo' and where it lived on to a ripe old age.

THE SQUARE, TURRIFF.   B. 361.

Youth leaders from Turriff's main organisations being presented with trophies by Turriff Town Council in 1966. Rear L-R: Provost G. Riddoch Wood, James Peppiette (Boy Scouts), Bill Sinclair (Army Cadets), James Chrystall (Air Cadets), Alex Brown (Boys Brigade), Adam Simpson (Town Clerk of Turriff). Front (L-R) Kathleen Donald (Girl Guides), Sandra Davidson (Brownies), Aileen Ingram (Wolf Cubs), Mary Bruce (Life Boys), Peg Davidson (Women's Junior Air Corps).

Commonwealth Youth Sunday May 1958 led by Turriff Silver Band. This was an annual event and the large turnout was due to the large number of young people in the town who were born immediately after the Second World War. A rough estimate would suggest that about 180 boys and girls attended the service that day.

Threshing at Lendrum, Auchterless in the late 1920s. The mill is driven by a Titan tractor, farmer was Robert Paterson of "Turra Coo" fame

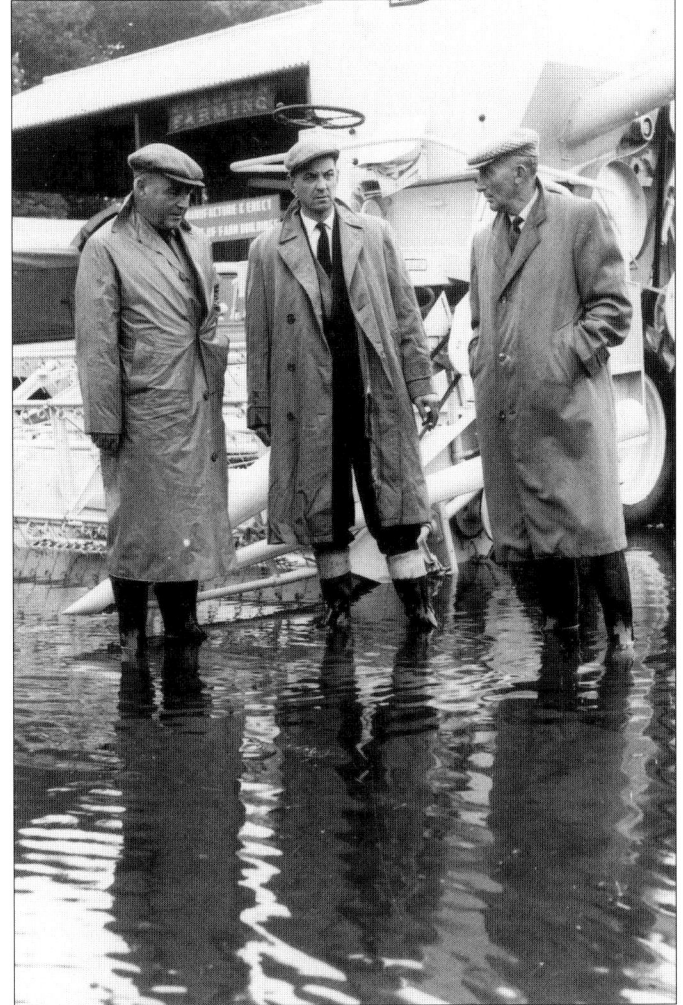

Turriff Show 1962 (Another wet one!)

Wallace McIntosh (centre), salesman for Barclay Ross & Hutchison, on their stand at Turriff Show with two potential customers. Possibly a bulk purchase of wellies?

Two new projects have come to fruition during the Millennium Year. The old facade of Turriff Central Mart arch has finally found a permanent home as gateway to the east entrance of the Den in Crown Street. Turriff Community Council and helpers including Willie Davidson and Stanley Duguid are to be congratulated on a job well done. In High Street, the millennium map organised by the Rotary Club has been completed and forms a fitting backdrop to the flower beds. By popular request more benches have been added, where the local worthies enjoy a seat in the sun, while watching the world go by. Millennium map photograph L-R – Peter Robertson, Bill Stronach, Dick Hutcheon, Douglas Hay, Bert Connon, Leslie Simpson, George Kennedy, George Cruickshank.

Turriff and District Heritage Society was formed in 1979, the inaugural committee were, president, Miss E. Cormack, vice president Mrs H. Penny, joint secretaries Mrs D. Smith and Mr G. Hay, treasurer Mr G. Berstan.

Their first museum was a cottage off Castle Street which was the former home of the session clerk of the Auld Kirk behind the Cross. It was renamed Session Cottage Museum and the society laid it out to depict a 'but and ben' cottage at the end of the nineteenth century.

Today the society have two museums, Session Cottage and the former Turriff Post Office which has been renamed The Auld Post Office Museum.

Fund-raising is currently in progress for the purchase of a sealed display cabinet for the civic robes and regalia of the former Turriff Town Council. The robes are currently in the care of Aberdeenshire Council and it is hoped they can be returned to the museum in time for next year's opening in April 2001.

The first photograph shows the official opening of Turriff and District Heritage Society's Session Cottage Museum by Professor Alexander Fenton on 9th April 1983.

L-R – Councillor B. Mair, Mr G. Berstan, Mrs B. Dempster, Mrs D. Smith, Mr A Stephen, Miss A. E. Cormack, Professor Fenton, Mrs E. Fenton, Councillor H. Sim, Captain Hay of Delgatie, Mrs H. Penny.

The second photograph was taken in 1992 at the presentation of the Museum and Galleries Registration Certificate to the Trustees of Turriff and District Heritage Society.

L-R–(rear) Mrs E. McAllion, Mr H. Henshaw, Miss D. McAinsh, (front) Mr D. Cameron, Miss A.E. Cormack, Mr J. Chrystall.

Acknowledgements

I wish to thank Turriff and District Heritage Society for giving me the opportunity to write this book.

In particular James Chrystall, Honorary President and Dorothy Smith, Minute Secretary of the Society for allowing me access to the vast knowledge they have of their native Turriff.

Alan Cruickshank copied many of our photographs at no cost to the Society, for which they are very grateful.

To all who gave further information and loaned photographs, it was much appreciated.

W. D. Peters & Son must also be congratulated on their expertise in producing the book.

Last but not least, my sincere thanks to Duncan Cameron, Honorary Treasurer of the Society. Without the advice, help and encouragement I have had from Duncan this book would never have come to print.

Bill Simpson

Bibliography

Turriff Golf Club 1896-1996. N. K. Wilson

Two Hundred Years in St Ninian's and Forglen, Turriff. 1795-1995

Turriff Free Church, Laying of Memorial Stone. Banffshire Journal, July 1899 and June 1900

St Congan's (Turriff) Bazaar Album 1905

King Edward, Aberdeenshire, The Story of a Parish. James Godsman 1952. "Francie Markis"

Banffshire Journal 1906. "Cockie" and "Rabbitie Jamie"

The Kirks of the Turriff Presbytery 1904. The Old Church, Turriff

The Third Statistical Account of Scotland 1966. Turriff Higher Grade School

Banffshire Field Club. Talk by Dr W. Douglas Simpson 1936 on the Estate of Carnousie. The New House of Carnousie

Banff & Buchan. An Illustrated Guide. Chas. McKean 1990. Muiresk House

Banff & Buchan. An Illustrated Guide. Chas. McKean 1990. Dunlugas House.

Buchan. John B. Pratt, L.L.D. 4th Edition 1901. Hatton Castle.

Buchan. John B. Pratt, L.L.D. 4th Edition 1901. Delgatie Castle.

Buchan. John B. Pratt, L.L.D. 4th Edition 1901. Craigston Castle

Aberdeen University, George Washington Wilson Photographic Archive. Photograph of Clydesdale Bank, Turriff